Diet recommendations for Heart insufficiency

Please check these recommendations always with a nutrition consultant, therapist, doctor or dietician. The recipes and the list of ingredients are supporting the conventional medical therapy.
The calorie disclosures of fresh ingredients (fruit and vegetables) vary according to quality and time of harvest. The contents were checked by a dietician and a nutrition consultant for the Traditional Chinese Medicine (TCM).

Author:
©2017 Josef Miligui
www.ebns.at

AF200085

Source:
The lists are created from the EBNS database for nutritional counseling. The database is used by dietitians, therapists and doctors for advising the patient / client.

Literature:
The specialist literature and the training documents of the German and Austrian dietary and traditional Chinese medicine serve as a knowledge base. We have used the documents as a basis of knowledge, adapted it to our experience and completed them.
http://di-book.com

Title Photo:
©2008 Erika Weixlbaumer

Production and publishing:
BoD – Books on Demand, Norderstedt
ISBN 9783746043913

Diet recommendations for DIETETICS - Metabolism - Heart and circulation - Herat insufficiency

1 Treatment strategy

With low-salt diet and with the recommended amount of drinking by the doctor, the therapy can be optimally supported.
Reduce sodium levels,
Increase potassium levels.
You can also use fresh herbs instead of salt.
Stabilize Blood fat and cholesterol levels.
Drink sufficient but not too much.
Prefer banana, potatoes, fruit juices, nuts, seeds, chocolate, spinach, rucola, mushrooms, chestnuts.

2 Avoid

Salty food and dishes.

3 Breakfast

	kkal. per serving
Barley soup	265
Beet salad with salad cucumber	245
Black beans with avocado	263
Bulgur with tomatoes and fresh herbs	205
Carrot soup	209
Cereal fruit pulp	175
Compote from rhubarb	48
Couscous Salad	338
Creamy potatoes with cauliflower	332

4 Snack

5 Lunch

6   Afternoon

7 Dinner

8 Any time

9   Recipes

(recommended) = You can use more.
(little) = You should use less than specified or omit.

9.1   Avocado with lemon

Good to fight insomnia, inflammation, swelling, pain and itching. Is calming.
Cooking time approx. 5 min
Calories p. portion: 289
1 portions
Allergens: -

Quantity of ingredients
Avocado 1/2 piece / 120g. (recommended)
Lemon juice 1/2 piece / 10g. (yes)
Salt 1 pinch / 1g. (little)

Cooking instructions:
Halve the avocado, remove the core, add the lemon juice, salt a little and eat with a spoon.

9.2   Barley soup

Diuretic, forcing spleen, supports urination, stimulates liver function, antioxidativ, promotes digestion, detoxifying, reduces blood lipids, stimulates, dissolves stagnation.
Cooking time approx. 25 min
Calories p. portion: 265
2 portions
Allergens: A

Quantity of ingredients
Barley 1 cup / 120g. (yes)
Salt 1 pinch / 1g. (little)
Ginger fresh 1/2 teaspoon / 1g. (yes)
Olive oil 1 table spoon / 10g. (yes)
Parsley 2 table spoons / 30g. (yes)
Water 1 1/2 cups / 240g. (yes)

Cooking instructions:
Roast the barley in the pan, then grind it to the ground, and boil with water, some salt and ginger to a mash. Before serving add oil and parsley.
Variant: You can add a better taste to the dish if you cook it with prepared vegetable or meat broth.

9.3   Basic recipe for a reissue soup (Congee)

Low fat content, for the drainage of the body overweight and high blood pressure.
Cooking time approx. 2-4 hours
Calories p. portion: 140
3 portions
Allergens: -

Quantity of ingredients
Rice variety any 1 cup / 120g. (yes)
Water 6 cups / 700g. (yes)

Cooking instructions:
Cook rice and water in a ratio of about 1: 6. The amount of water determines the thickness of the mash (matter of taste).
Put the rice in a saucepan with a heavy lid. It is important to simmer the rice after a short boil on the slightest flame, otherwise it burns.
Boil the rice for 2-4 hours. The longer he cooks, the more he strengthens.
If you want to eat the dish for breakfast, you can put the rice on just before bedtime.
To be on the safe side, you should first check the behavior of your pot and cooker under observation for a similar
amount of time, so that nothing burns.
Refrigerate for later use.

9.4   Basic recipe for a vegetable soup, nutritious

Reduces blood pressure, strengthens immune system, prevents cancer, forcing spleen, dissolves stagnation, promotes weight loss. Good to fight immunodeficiency, high blood pressure, depressions, diabetes, diarrhea, reduces blood lipids.
Cooking time approx. 2-3 hours
Calories p. portion: 48
5 portions
Allergens: L

Quantity of ingredients
Olive oil 1 table spoon / 4g. (yes)
Onion white 1 piece / 60g. (yes)
Carrot 3 pieces / 200g. (yes)
Parsnip 3/8 lbs - 6oz / 150g. (recommended)
Celery root 1 cup / 100g. (yes)
Ginger fresh 1/2 teaspoon / 2g. (yes)
Lemon 1/2 piece / 25g. (yes)
Juniper berry 6 pieces / 6g. (yes)
Thyme dried 1 pinch / 1g. (yes)
Lovage 1 table spoon / 3g. (yes)
Bay leaf 2 leaves / 1g. (yes)
Salt 1 pinch / 1g. (little)
Water 3 cups / 650g. (yes)

Cooking instructions:
Cut the vegetables into cubes.
Heat oil in hot pot, fry shortly onions and vegetables.
Add cold water, then add ginger, bay leaf and lemon juice.
Season with juniper, thyme and lovage. Cover for 2 - 3 hours on a low heat and simmer.
The used vegetables should be thrown away.
The basic recipe serves as a soup base and to refine vegetables, legumes or cereals.
If you want to eat vegetable soup immediately, add the desired vegetables half an hour before.
Refrigerate for later use.

9.5   Beet salad with salad cucumber

Diuretic, detoxifying, suppresses conversion of sugar into fat, lowers cholesterol. Improves blood circulation, strengthens the muscles, antioxidativ. Strengthens gastrointestinal function, expands blood vessels, bactericide.
Cooking time approx. 45 min
Calories p. portion: 246
2 portions
Allergens: GMO

Quantity of ingredients
Red beet 4 pieces / 200g. (yes)
Cucumber 1 piece / 250g. (yes)
Olive oil 4 table spoons / 40g. (yes)
Sugar cane sugar 1 pinch / 1g. (little)
Pepper (ground) 1 pinch / 0,2g. (yes)
Mustard seeds 1 pinch of powder / 0,2g. (yes)
Dill 1/2 teaspoon (chopped) / 2g. (yes)
Onion (spring onion) 2 pieces / 40g. (yes)
Salt 1 pinch / 0,5g. (little)
Vinegar (Apple vinegar) 1 dach / 1g. (yes)
Sour cream 15% fat 2 table spoons / g. (little)
Pepper powder (hot) 1 pinch / 0,3g. (yes)

Cooking instructions:
Softly boil beetroot, peel and dice; Peel and dice the cucumber.
Dressing: olive oil, a little whole cane sugar, pepper, mustard powder,
dill, finely chopped spring onion, salt, vinegar, a little sour cream and a
pinch of rose paprika; stir; mix with the beetroot and let it rest; Add the
cucumbers just before serving to keep their light color. Serve with:
millet, which together with the salad makes a simple, light meal.

9.6   Beetroot soup

Strengthens gastrointestinal function, expands blood vessels,
strengthens the muscles, antioxidativ. Promotes digestion, dissolves
stagnation.
Cooking time approx. 20-30 min
Calories p. portion: 282
4 portions
Allergens: G

Quantity of ingredients
Olive oil 2 table spoons / 20g. (yes)
Onion white 1 piece chopped / 50g. (yes)
Garlic 1 clove / 2g. (yes)
Red beet 2,2 lbs (Peeled and diced) / 1000g. (yes)
Cumin (Caraway seed) 1 table spoon / 7g. (yes)
Curcuma 1 teaspoon / 2g. (yes)
Oregano fresh 1 pinch of fresh / 2g. (yes)
Peppers (rose peppers) 1 teaspoon / 2g. (yes)
Crème fraiche cheese 1/4 lbs - 4oz / 125g. (little)

Cooking instructions:
Heat the oil in a saucepan, fry the onions and garlic in dark brown. Add cumin, turmeric, oregano and salt and deglaze with 1 liter of water. Cook the beetroot for about 20 minutes. Puree the soup and serve in soup bowls with 1 tbsp. creme fraiche. Finally, sprinkle the rose pepper over it.

9.7 Beetroot soup with sauerkraut potato biscuits

Promotes spleen and liver, reduces blood pressure, strengthens immune system. Improves digestion, regenerates skin, supports urination, lowers cholesterol. Little laxative.
Cooking time approx. 30 min
Calories p. portion: 128
2 portions
Allergens: GLN

Quantity of ingredients
Red beet 1/4 lbs - 4oz / 125g. (yes)
Potato 1 oz / 25g. (recommended)
Basic recipe for a vegetable soup (nutritious) 1 cup / 250g. (yes)
Lemon juice 1/4 / 6g. (yes)
Salt 1 pinch / 0,5g. (little)
Sesame oil 1/2 teaspoon / 1g. (yes)
Potato 1/8 lbs - 2oz / 50g. (recommended)
Butter Bio 1 teaspoon / 10g. ()
Sauerkraut (cutted cabbage fermented) 1 oz / 25g. (yes)
Cream sour 10% 1 teaspoon / 3g. (yes)
Sesame, white 1 teaspoon / 2g. (recommended)
Marjoram 1 pinch / 0,3g. (yes)
Salt 1 pinch / 0,5g. (little)

Cooking instructions:
Peel beetroot and potatoes and cut into small cubes, heat till it boils, add sesame oil and lemon juice and simmer for 20 minutes until the beetroot is tender.
For the cookies, the potatoes are peeled, cut into thin slices and buttered. Bake at 200°C/392°F in the oven for 1/4 hour until golden. Sweat finely chopped sauerkraut in butter, add sour cream, marjoram and salt. This mass is distributed on the potato slices, sprinkled with

sesame seeds and baked for a few minutes at 200°C/392°F.
Puree the soup and season with salt and cream. Serve the finished
soup with the sauerkraut and potato cookies.

9.8   Black beans with avocado

Anti-inflammatory, good to fight swelling and pain. Supports urination,
lowers cholesterol, prevents arteriosclerosis, improves blood circulation,
strengthens the muscles. Promotes digestion, detoxifying, promotes
perspiration, reduces blood lipids, stimulates, dissolves stagnation.
Cooking time approx. 1 hour
Calories p. portion: 264
3 portions
Allergens: EN

Quantity of ingredients
Black beans 1 cup / 100g. (yes)
Water 4 cups / 450g. (yes)
Lemon 1 dash / 1g. (yes)
Boxhorn clover seeds 1 pinch (powder) / 0,2g. (yes)
Sesame oil 1 table spoon / 10g. (yes)
Ginger fresh 1 teaspoon / 2g. (yes)
Wakame 1 inch / 1g. (yes)
Soy sauce 1 dash / 1g. (yes)
Avocado 1 piece / 300g. (recommended)

Cooking instructions:
Preparation the day before:
Soak 2 cups of black beans in about 6 cups of cold water for 6-8 hours
and then strain.
Put the black beans in 4 cups of fresh cold water; add a dash of lemon
juice, some fenugreek seed powder, 1 tablespoon of sesame oil, 1
teaspoon of grated ginger; add a piece of wakame or 1 tbsp of Hijiki.
Simmer for about 45 minutes; puree with the blender; season with
plenty of soy sauce.

In the morning:
Peel ½ avocado per serving and cut into small boats; Serve with the
warm bean paste.

Note: The black beans can be pre-cooked for 2 - 3 days to be used as
breakfast or other meals with little effort.

9.9 Bulgur with tomatoes and fresh herbs

Promotes digestion, helps to digest fat, supports urination, reduces blood pressure. Stimulates digestion, supports urination.
Cooking time approx. 30 min
Calories p. portion: 205
1 portions
Allergens: A

Quantity of ingredients
Bulgur (cereals) 1 cup / 120g. (yes)
Tomato 2 pieces / 70g. (yes)
Rucola 2 table spoons / 16g. (recommended)
Pepper powder (hot) 1 pinch / 2g. (yes)
Olive oil 2 table spoons / 20g. (yes)
Pepper (ground) 1 pinch / 0,5g. (yes)
Salt 1 pinch / 1g. (little)
Basil 4 leaves / 2g. (yes)
Thyme 1 Twig / 3g. (yes)
Lemon juice 1/2 piece / 10g. (yes)

Cooking instructions:
Put cold water in a pot, sprinkle in Bulgur and simmer. Stir in chopped tomatoes, fresh herbs like basil, thyme, arugula, a pinch of rose paprika, lemon juice, a dash of olive oil, a little ground pepper, some salt.

Variant: add some mozzarella.
Recommendation: ideal morning meal in summer; also suitable as evening meal, especially for sleep disorders.

9.10 Carrot soup

Promotes spleen and liver, reduces blood pressure, strengthens immune system, prevents cancer, reduces radiation damage, improves blood circulation, improves medication effect, increase Appetite, stimulates liver function.
Cooking time approx. 30 min
Calories p. portion: 210
2 portions
Allergens: O

Quantity of ingredients
Carrot 1,1 lbs / 500g. (yes)
Pepper (ground) 1 pinch / 0,5g. (yes)
Nutmeg 1 pinch / 1g. (yes)
Salt 1 pinch / 1g. (little)
White wine 1/2 cup / 125g. (little)
Orange juice Alternatively for wine / g. (little)
Parsley 2 table spoons / 10g. (yes)
Peppers powder 1 pinch / 1g. (yes)
Thyme dried Alternative to rose paprika / g. (yes)
Pine nuts 1 table spoon / 15g. (recommended)
Sunflower seeds Alternatively to pine nuts / g. (recommended)

Cooking instructions:
Place peeled large cut carrot pieces in hot water; cook and then puree; season with ground pepper, a little nutmeg, a pinch of salt; add a dash of white wine and simmer for a few minutes or season with orange juice; Add parsley as desired;
stir in some rose paprika or fresh thyme; sprinkle with roasted pine nuts or sunflower seeds before serving.

9.11 Cereal fruit pulp

Lots of vitamin C, strengthens immune system, antiparasitic.
Cooking time approx. 10 min
Calories p. portion: 175
1 portions
Allergens: A

Quantity of ingredients
Oat flakes (whole grain) 1/2 oz / 20g. (yes)
Water 3,5 oz / 90g. (yes)
Apple juice (natural cloudy) 1/4 lbs - 4oz / 100g. (recommended)
Rapeseed oil 1/8 oz / 5g. (yes)

Cooking instructions:
Heat the water till it boils the add the cereals. Instant flakes you only need to mix with hot water. Stir fruit juice or puree and grease. The fresh fruit (for example, apples, pears, peaches) can be raw or kneaded. Frozen fruit or industrially produced fruit jars without added sugar are also suitable. Bananas should be mixed with less sweet fruit.

9.12 Champignon soup with red wine

Promotes digestion and is good to fight high blood pressure. For strengthening after diseases, for calming and sleeping, as pain killers, mood brightening, cardiovascular disorders, against fullness. Sleep disorders: without red wine.
Cooking time approx. 15 min
Calories p. portion: 269
2 portions
Allergens: CGNO

Quantity of ingredients
Sesame oil 2 table spoons / 20g. (yes)
Champignon 1 1/2 cups / 250g. (recommended)
Pepper (ground) 1 pinch / 0,2g. (yes)
Salt 1 pinch / 1g. (little)
Sour cream 15% fat 2 table spoons / 20g. (little)
Red wine 2oz / 125g. (little)
Sugar cane sugar 1 pinch / 1g. (little)
Chicken yolk 2 pieces / 40g. (yes)
Nutmeg 1 pinch / 0,3g. (yes)
Parsley 2 table spoons (chopped) / 20g. (yes)

Cooking instructions:
Sauté briefly fry sliced mushrooms in sesame oil in a hot pot. Add pepper, salt, plenty of sour cream, hot water, a good shot of red wine; simmer for a few minutes; add a pinch of whole cane sugar, 1 egg yolk, nutmeg; season with salt; stir in fresh parsley.

9.13 Chicory salad with oranges and grapefruit

Mineral supporter and is full of A-B-C vitamins. Promotes digestion, relieves alcohol poisoning, lowers blood glucose. Promotes digestion.
Cooking time approx. 10 min
Calories p. portion: 236
1 portions
Allergens:

Quantity of ingredients
Chicory 1/4 lbs - 4oz / 120g. (yes)
Orange 1 piece / 100g. (yes)
Grapefruit (Pomelo) 1/2 piece / 100g. (yes)
Onion white 1 smal / 30g. (yes)
Lemon juice 2 table spoons / 20g. (yes)
Pepper (ground) 1 pinch / 0,2g. (yes)
Ginger powder 1 pinch / 0,2g. (yes)
Sugar candy white 1 knife tip / 0,5g. (little)
Orange grated peel 1 teaspoon / 2g. (yes)
Olive oil 1 table spoon / 10g. (yes)

Cooking instructions:
Wash chicory and cut it to size. Peel and fillet oranges and grapefruit. Mix with the chicory. From lemon juice, salt, pepper, ginger, sugar, chopped onion and oil stir a sauce. Mix chicory, orange fillets and sauce. Sprinkle the salad with orange peel rasps.

9.14 Compote from rhubarb

Antipyretic, analgesic, detoxifying, bactericide.
Cooking time approx. 15 min
Calories p. portion: 48
1 portions
Allergens:

Quantity of ingredients
Rhubarb 1/4 lbs - 4oz / 100g. (yes)
Water 1 cup / 120g. (yes)
Honey 1 table spoon / 10g. (little)

Cooking instructions:
Wash rhubarb and cut small. Boil in the water. Allow to cool a little and add the honey.

9.15 Couscous Salad

prevents cancer, forcing spleen, promotes digestion, stimulates liver function, reduces blood pressure, strengthens immune system, reduces radiation damage, diuretic.
Cooking time approx. 25 min
Calories p. portion: 338
3 portions
Allergens: A

Quantity of ingredients
Water 1 cup / 100g. (yes)
Olive oil 1 table spoon / 15g. (yes)
Couscous 5/8 oz / 200g. (yes)
Lemon juice 2 table spoons / 30g. (yes)
Lemon peel 1 teaspoon / 2g. (yes)
Tomato 2 pieces / 80g. (yes)
Cucumber 1/4 lbs - 4oz / 100g. (yes)
Carrot 1/4 lbs - 4oz / 100g. (yes)
Parsley 1 Bunch / 100g. (yes)
Chives 1 Bunch / 100g. (yes)
Peppermint 3 twigs / 30g. (yes)

Cooking instructions:
Boil in a small saucepan 250 ml. water with salt and 1 tablespoon olive oil. Add the couscous, take the stove in the front and let it swell covered for 5 minutes. Put the couscous back on the stove and let it simmer for about 2 minutes with gentle stirring. If necessary, add 1 - 3 tbsp of hot water.
Mix the couscous with lemon juice, chopped lemon peel and 1 tbsp oil, season with salt and pepper and leave to set.
Add couscous with tomatoes, cucumber, parsley (all diced), carrots (grated), chives and mint (finely chopped).
Season the couscous salad with lemon juice, salt and pepper.

9.16 Creamy potatoes with cauliflower

Improves digestion, regenerates skin, supports urination, lowers cholesterol, stimulates liver function, detoxifying.
Cooking time approx. 30 min
Calories p. portion: 332
1 portions
Allergens: CG

Quantity of ingredients
Potato 3/8 lbs - 6oz / 150g. (recommended)
Cauliflower 1/8 lbs - 2oz / 50g. (yes)
Cow's milk (whole milk 3.5% fat) 2 table spoons / 30g. (yes)
Cream, sweet 30% 1 table spoon / 10g. (little)
Butter organic 1 teaspoon / 10g. ()
Parsley 1 teaspoon / 3g. (yes)
Chicken yolk 1 piece / 25g. (yes)

Cooking instructions:
Wash the potatoes under running water, thoroughly wash the cauliflower in stagnant water.
Divide the cauliflower florets into small buds, cut the stems into pieces about 1 cm in size.
Peel the potatoes and cut into 2 cm cubes.
Heat the milk with the cream in a saucepan, add the potatoes and the cauliflower. Cook on low heat for about 15 minutes.
Put the vegetables in a plate, add the butter, the chopped parsley and the egg yolk and lightly knead and mix everything with a fork.

9.17 Cucumber salad

Diuretic, detoxifying, suppresses conversion of sugar into fat, lowers cholesterol, prevents cancer. Cucumber cools and moistens. Dill works against flatulence, anticonvulsant in gastrointestinal discomfort.
Cooking time approx. 5 min
Calories p. portion: 27
2 portions
Allergens: O

Quantity of ingredients
Cucumber 1 piece / 400g. (yes)
Salt 1 pinch / 1g. (little)
Dill 1 pinch / 1g. (yes)
Vinegar (Apple vinegar) 1 table spoon / 10g. (yes)

Cooking instructions:
Cut the cucumber (do not peel when organic) thinly and season.

9.18 Fast polenta with avocado and spring onion

Good to fight inflammations, swelling, pain. Forcing spleen and stomach, lets urine and bile juice flow, dissolves stagnation. Includes unsaturated fatty acids, antioxidativ.
Cooking time approx. 10 min
Calories p. portion: 450
2 portions
Allergens:

Quantity of ingredients
Corn (fast polenta) 1 cup / 120g. (yes)
Water 1 1/2 cups / 240g. (yes)
Olive oil 1 table spoon / 15g. (yes)
Salt 1 pinch / 1g. (little)
Pepper (ground) 1 pinch / 0,5g. (yes)
Lemon juice 1 dash / 3g. (yes)
Onion (spring onion) 2 pieces / 40g. (yes)
Avocado 1/2 piece / 150g. (recommended)
Turmeric (yellow root) 1 pinch / 1g. (yes)
Basil (fresh) 1 teaspoon / 2g. (yes)

Cooking instructions:
Heat water, add oil, lemon and spices.
When the water boils, add the polenta while stirring constantly and cook for 2 minutes.
When the porridge becomes firm, the polenta is ready.
Add diced avocado and sliced spring onion to the polenta. Sprinkle fresh basil on it.

9.19 Fennel with roasted walnuts

Forcing spleen, detoxifying, reduces inflammation, improves blood circulation, improves medication effect, stimulates appetite, antioxidativ, promotes digestion, stimulates, dissolves stagnation.
Cooking time approx. 20 min
Calories p. portion: 342
4 portions
Allergens: HO

Quantity of ingredients
Fennel 4 pieces / 800g. (yes)
Nutmeg 1 pinch / 1g. (yes)
Ginger fresh 1/2 teaspoon / 1g. (yes)
Salt 1 pinch / 1g. (little)
White wine 1/2 cup / 125g. (little)
Peppers powder 1 pinch / 1g. (yes)
Olive oil 2 table spoons / 40g. (yes)
Walnuts 2 table spoons / 35g. (recommended)
Water 1 1/2 cups / 220g. (yes)
Corn Grease (Polenta) 1 cup / 120g. (yes)
Salt 1 pinch / 1g. (little)

Cooking instructions:
Heat very little water in a pot; Fry the fennel in strips. Add Nutmeg, a little grated ginger, add salt, a dash of white wine, rose paprika. Simmer until the vegetables are cooked, but still crisp; stir in a little olive oil; sprinkle with roasted walnuts.

Stir the polenta into a pot of hot water, stirring constantly, until the polenta has the desired consistency. Salt.
Pull the polenta off the fire and let it swell for about 10 minutes.

9.20 Grated apple

Eat 3 times a day - Apple (sour) scraped and brown is stuffing. Relieves diarrhea.
Cooking time approx. 10 min
Calories p. portion: 120
1 portions
Allergens:

Quantity of ingredients
Apple (sour) 1 piece / 200g. (yes)

Cooking instructions:
Peel apple and grate as fine as possible. Leave for at least 5 minutes until it turns brown.

9.21 Grated carrots with apple

Promotes spleen and liver, reduces blood pressure, strengthens immune system, prevents cancer, reduces radiation damage, stops diarrhea, promotes digestion, appetizing, harmonizes the stomach.
Cooking time approx. 10 min
Calories p. portion: 74
1 portions
Allergens:

Quantity of ingredients
Carrot 1/4 lbs - 4oz / 100g. (yes)
Apple (sweet) 1 piece / 50g. (yes)
Lemon juice 2 teaspoons / 3g. (yes)
Sugar substitute (sweetener) 1g. Or 0,034oz / 1g. (yes)

Cooking instructions:
Mix lemon juice with sweetener. Grate the washed, thinly peeled carrots and the apple piece into the sauce and mix.

9.22 Grilled salmon steaks with cauliflower and potatoes

Improves digestion, regenerates skin, supports urination, lowers cholesterol, supports digestion.
Cooking time approx. 30 min
Calories p. portion: 330
4 portions
Allergens: D

Quantity of ingredients
Garlic 1 clove / 1g. (yes)
Onion (shallot) 1/2 piece / 5g. (yes)
Lemon juice 1 dash / 1g. (yes)
Salt 1 pinch / 1g. (little)
Cauliflower 1 piece / 500g. (yes)
Olive oil 2 table spoons / 20g. (yes)
Garlic 1 clove / 1g. (yes)
Water 2/3 cup / g. (yes)
Parsley 2 table spoons / 15g. (yes)
Potato 1,1 lbs / 500g. (recommended)
Salt 1 pinch / 1g. (little)
Salmon 4 pieces (steaks) / 500g. (yes)
Lemon 1/2 piece / 2g. (yes)

Cooking instructions:
Garlic shallots mixture:
Finely squeeze the garlic, finely chop the shallots, add a dash of lemon juice and salt and stir. Mix with a little oil to a paste.

Cauliflower:
Cut the cauliflower into pieces.
Heat the oil in a heavy saucepan and fry the crushed garlic for a short time.
Add the cauliflower pieces and turn in the oil. Add a little water and cook until the cauliflower is firm. Strain the cauliflower and cook the remaining water until a thick sauce remains. Add the cauliflower and

crush it roughly with a wooden spoon. Add the chopped parsley and salt.

Potatoes:
Cook the potato in a saucepan with plenty of water, strain and peel.

Salmon Steak:
Preheat the oven at about 180°C/356°F. Rub in the salmon slices with the garlic-scarlet mixture and grill as close as possible to the heat source for 4 to 8 minutes from both sides. You are done when the meat is easy to divide when you pierce with a fork.

Serve and sprinkle with lemon slices and the chopped parsley.

9.23 Italian Vegetable and Bean Soup

Promotes digestion, helps to digest fat, supports urination, reduces blood pressure. Stimulates blood production and metabolism, reduces fat, reduces blood pressure, strengthens immune system.
Cooking time approx. 1 hour
Calories p. portion: 204
4 portions
Allergens: L

Quantity of ingredients
Butter beans white 5/8 oz / 200g. (yes)
Onion (shallot) 1 piece / 20g. (yes)
Carrot 1 piece / 70g. (yes)
Olive oil 2 table spoons / 20g. (yes)
Tomato 2 pieces / 80g. (yes)
Celery root 1/4 lbs / 100g. (yes)
White cabbage 0,2 lbs / 70g. (yes)
Endive salad 1/8 lbs - 2oz / 50g. (yes)
Salt 1 pinch / 1g. (little)
Pepper (ground) 1 pinch / 0,2g. (yes)
Water 2 cup / 450g. (yes)

Cooking instructions:
Soak beans and cook for 1/2 hour.
Fry onions, carrots and celery in frying oil.
Add tomatoes and water and simmer for 30 minutes.
Cut white cabbage into strips. Add the cabbage and endive salad and the boiled beans, and season with salt, pepper and olive oil.

9.24 Kohlrabi in curry sauce with potatoes

Reduces inflammation, lowers cholesterol, diuretic, conducts bowel winds, strengthens immune system, prevents cancer, promotes weight loss. Good to fight loss of appetite, flatulence, high blood pressure, depressions, diabetes, diarrhea.
Cooking time approx. 1 hour
Calories p. portion: 188
4 portions
Allergens: GL

Quantity of ingredients
Potato 6 pieces / 450g. (recommended)
Basic recipe for a vegetable soup (nutritious) 1 cup / 300g. (yes)
Potato 1/4 lbs - 4oz / 100g. (recommended)
Nutmeg 1 pinch / 0,2g. (yes)
Lemon peel 1/2 teaspoon / 2g. (yes)
Ginger fresh 1/2 teaspoon / 2g. (yes)
Lovage 1/2 teaspoon / 2g. (yes)
Kohlrabi 3/4 lbs / 300g. (yes)
Salt 1 pinch / 1g. (little)
Pepper (ground) 1 pinch / 0,2g. (yes)
Sour cream 15% fat 2 table spoons / 30g. (little)
Chervil dried 1 Bunch / 80g. (yes)

Cooking instructions:
Boil the potatoes in salted water.
Bring half of the vegetable stock to boil. Add the diced potatoes, nutmeg, lemon zest, ginger and lovage. Cover the potatoes and cook for about 10 minutes until soft and puree them with a blender until they are smooth.
Bring remaining vegetable stock to boil. Cut kohlrabi into cubes and add, cover and cook for about 8 minutes. Stir in the potato sauce and heat everything briefly.
Puree with the mixing stick chervil and sour cream. Mix the chervil cream with the kohlrabi vegetables.
Serve with the cooked, peeled potatoes.

9.25 Lettuce with vinegar dressing

Relieves fatigue, regulates gastrointestinal function, dissolves stagnation, laxative, antiparasitic, improves blood circulation, detoxifying, reduces inflammation, relieves pain.
Cooking time approx. 10 min
Calories p. portion: 68
2 portions
Allergens: O

Quantity of ingredients
Lettuce 1 piece / 200g. (recommended)
Vinegar (Apple vinegar) 1 table spoon / 10g. (yes)
Water 1 table spoon / 10g. (yes)
Rapeseed oil 1 table spoon / 10g. (yes)
Onion (spring onion) 1 piece / 20g. (yes)
Salt 1 pinch / 0,5g. (little)
Pepper (ground) 1 pinch / 0,1g. (yes)
Chives 1 table spoon / 5g. (yes)

Cooking instructions:
Clean lettuce, wash and drain. Add the ingredients to the marinade in an extra container. Salad with marinade just before consumption. Just before, sprinkle with chives.

9.26 Mango banana yoghurt drink ice cold

Good to fight loss of appetite, oral mucosa inflammation. Regulates gastrointestinal function, chronic constipation. Prevents cancer. Diuretic, forcing spleen.
Cooking time approx. 5 min
Calories p. portion: 121
2 portions
Allergens: G

Quantity of ingredients
Mango juice 1/2 cup / 100g. (recommended)
Yogurt (natural, 1.5% fat) 1/4 lbs - 4oz / 100g. (yes)
Mineral water 1/2 cup / 100g. (yes)
Banana 1/2 piece / 150g. (recommended)
Acerola fruit nectar or powder 1 teaspoon / 2g. (little)

Cooking instructions:
Mix all the ingredients and 2-3 ice cubes in a blender.

9.27 Millet with shiitake mushrooms and avocado

Anti-inflammatory, good to fight swelling and pain, promotes spleen and kidney, diuretic, stimulates digestion, building up, eye-enhancing, detoxifying, nerve-strengthening, building up.
Cooking time approx. 20 min
Calories p. portion: 560
2 portions
Allergens: G

Quantity of ingredients
Millet 1 cup / 120g. (yes)
Water 1 1/2 cups / 200g. (yes)
Shiitake, dried 1 oz / 25g. (recommended)
Ginger fresh 1/2 teaspoon / 2g. (yes)
Pepper (ground) 1 pinch / 0,5g. (yes)
Salt 1 pinch / 1g. (little)
Parsley 1 table spoon / 7g. (yes)
Peppers powder 1 pinch / 1g. (yes)
Butter Bio 1 table spoon / 15g. ()
Avocado 1 piece / 200g. (recommended)
Lemon juice 1 dash / 3g. (yes)
Rucola 2 handful / 30g. (recommended)

Cooking instructions:
In a saucepan with hot water, sprinkle the millet, add in strips cut shiitake mushrooms and some ginger and simmer; add a pinch of ground pepper, a little salt, plenty of parsley, a pinch of rose pepper, stir in a piece of butter.
In the meantime: place ½ peeled avocado per serving on one half of the plate: sprinkle with a little ground pepper, a small pinch of salt; drizzle with lemon juice; sprinkle a little chopped rocket or rose paprika over it.
Put the millet dish on the other half of the plate.

9.28 Noodles with Vegetable and tomato sauce

Protects the digestive system. Detoxifying, Good to fight loss of appetite, flatulence, inflammatory bowel disease, obesity, gout, stomach ulcers, stomach cramps, rheumatism, heartburn, twelffinger intestinal ulcers, promotes digestion, helps to digest fat.
Cooking time approx. 45 min
Calories p. portion: 562
2 portions
Allergens: ACG

Quantity of ingredients
Tomato 1/4 lbs - 4oz / 125g. (yes)
Carrot 1 piece / 80g. (yes)
Zucchini 1 piece / 80g. (yes)
Olive oil 1 table spoon / 15g. (yes)
Onion (shallot) 1 piece / 20g. (yes)
Oregano dried 1 pinch / 1g. (yes)
Salt 1 pinch / 1g. (little)
Pepper (ground) 1 pinch / 0,2g. (yes)
Noodles (wheat) with egg 5/8 oz / 200g. (yes)
Olive oil 1 table spoon / 10g. (yes)
Crème fraiche cheese 2 table spoons / 30g. (little)

Cooking instructions:
Boil the tomatoes with a little water, drain and collect the juice, cut the tomatoes into pieces.
Roughly grate zucchini and carrot. Heat olive oil in a pot. Steam shallots very soft. Add tomatoes, season with oregano, salt and pepper. Simmer tomatoes to a thick sauce.
Bring plenty of salted water to boil, cook the wholegrain noodles until firm.
In the cooking time of the pasta, heat in a pan olive oil. Fry the carrots while stirring, lightly salt. Add zucchini, sauté briefly while stirring. The vegetables should be soft with a bite.
Drain pasta, mix with crème fraiche, season with salt and pepper. Garnish with the tomato sauce.

9.29 Oven potatoes with celery-curd cheese (quark)

Promotes spleen, reduces Inflammation, improves digestion, regenerates skin, supports urination, lowers cholesterol.
Cooking time approx. 30 min
Calories p. portion: 304
2 portions
Allergens: GL

Quantity of ingredients
Celery root 3 oz / 80g. (yes)
Basic recipe for a vegetable soup (nutritious) 1/2 cup / 100g. (yes)
Ground caraway 1 pinch / 0,2g. (yes)
Lemon peel 1/2 teaspoon / 1g. (yes)
Salt 1 pinch / 1g. (little)
Pepper (ground) 1 pinch / 0,2g. (yes)
Lemon juice 1 teaspoon / 3g. (yes)
Curd cheese 20% 5/8 oz / 200g. (yes)
Crème fraiche cheese 1/2 teaspoon / 5g. (little)
Potato 6 pieces / 400g. (recommended)
Olive oil 2 teaspoons / 5g. (yes)
Salt 1 pinch / 1g. (little)

Cooking instructions:
Celery-curd cheese:
Mix celery with vegetable broth according to basic recipe, caraway and lemon peel. Cook for about 8 minutes until the celery is soft and the vegetable broth almost evaporated. Mix the celery vegetable broth with the lemon juice, finely, and stir until smooth. Season with salt and pepper.
Baked potatoes:
Preheat oven to 200 °C / 400 °F.
Brush the potatoes well, halve them, and place them on a baking tray with the cut surface facing up. Lightly salt the surfaces and sprinkle with oil. Fry the potatoes in the oven for about 25 minutes.
Serve the celery plug to the potatoes.

9.30 Plums with curd cheese

Cancer preventive effect, dehydrates the body, stimulates digestion and binds fats in the intestine. Good to fight weakness, belching, diabetes, acute or chronic obstruction of the bowel, skin problems.
Cooking time approx. 10 min
Calories p. portion: 141
2 portions
Allergens: G

Quantity of ingredients
Plums 1 lbs / 500g. (yes)
Butter Bio 1/2 teaspoon / 2g. ()
Vanilla 1 pinch / 0,2g. (yes)
Cinnamon ground 1 pinch / 0,2g. (yes)
Coriander 1 pinch / 0,2g. (yes)
Cardamom 1 pinch / 0,2g. (yes)
Lemon juice 1 dash / 1g. (yes)
Cocoa 1 pinch / 0,3g. (yes)
Apple juice (natural cloudy) 1 dash / 3g. (recommended)
Sugar cane sugar 1 teaspoon / 3g. (little)
Curd cheese 20% 2 table spoons / 30g. (yes)

Cooking instructions:
Cut plums in half. Steam the plums in a pan in a little butter. Add vanilla, cinnamon and a pinch of cilantro and cardamom.
Add water so that the plums ¼ are covered.
Add lemon juice and a pinch of cocoa. Pour with little pear or apple juice, so that the plums are covered about halfway.
Sweet to taste with whole cane sugar.
Approximately Simmer for 7 minutes on the lightest heat so that the plums are tender but not overcooked.
Arrange plums in a circle on the plate.
In the middle a tablespoon of organic quark (who may like to use sheep milk quark).
Pour little juice of cooked plums over the dessert.

9.31 Porridge with cherries

Strengthens immune system. Improves blood circulation, reduces inflammation, moisturizer dry skin. Little laxative.
Cooking time approx. 10 min
Calories p. portion: 228
2 portions
Allergens: AG

Quantity of ingredients
Oat flakes (whole grain) 8 table spoons / 60g. (yes)
Water 1/2 cup / 125g. (yes)
Cow's milk (1.5% fat) 1/2 cup / 125g. (yes)
Salt 1 pinch / 0,2g. (little)
Cream, sweet 30% 2 table spoons / 20g. (little)
Sugar cane sugar 1 table spoon / 8g. (little)
Cherry 1/4 lbs - 4oz (gutted) / 100g. (yes)

Cooking instructions:
Heat water and milk and a pinch of salt till it boils. Sprinkle in 4 tablespoons of coarse rolled oats and cook to a pulp, add 4 tablespoons of fine oatmeal, allow to simmer. Arrange in a preheated bowl and top with cream. Core and add cherries.

9.32 Potato with dandelion salad

Promotes spleen, reduces inflammation, improves digestion, regenerates skin, supports urinating, lowers cholesterol, detoxifying, reduces inflammation, forcing spleen and digestive system, detoxifying, dissolves stagnation.
Cooking time approx. 25 min
Calories p. portion: 162
2 portions
Allergens:

Quantity of ingredients
Potato 5/8 lbs - 8oz / 250g. (recommended)
Onion white 1/2 piece / 20g. (yes)
Sunflower oil 1 table spoon / 10g. (yes)
Dandelion (young plants) 1/4 lbs - 4oz / 125g. (yes)
Salt 1 pinch / 1g. (little)
Pepper white (ground) 1 pinch / 0,5g. (yes)

Cooking instructions:
Cook the potatoes in salted water and cut into thin slices. Finely chop the onion. Now season the potatoes with oil, salt and pepper and add the dandelion and mix.

9.33 Potatoes with wild garlic-curd cheese

Improves digestion, regenerates skin, supports urination, lowers cholesterol. Helps to fight stomach pressure, belching, diabetes, acute or chronic constipation of the intestine. Improves the flow characteristics of the blood.
Cooking time approx. 20 min
Calories p. portion: 254
2 portions
Allergens: G

Quantity of ingredients
Potato 3/4 lbs / 300g. (recommended)
Salt 1 pinch / 0,1g. (little)
Wild garlic (garlic spinach) 2 handful / 30g. (yes)
Curd cheese 20% 5/8 lbs - 8oz / 250g. (yes)
Yogurt (natural, 1.5% fat) 2 table spoons / 20g. (yes)
Salt 1 pinch / 1g. (little)

Cooking instructions:
Cook potatoes in salted water and peel.
Wash he wild garlic leaves and carefully dried and cut into fine strips. Mix the cottage cheese, yogurt and salt and mix in the chopped wild garlic pieces. Serve with the potatoes.
In the season in which no wild garlic grows the wild garlic pesto can be used.

9.34 Provencal noodle pan

Improves blood circulation, reduces Inflammation, relieves pain, strengthens the muscles, tendons and bones, diuretic, supports urination.
Cooking time approx. 45 min
Calories p. portion: 196
2 portions
Allergens: ACL

Quantity of ingredients
Noodles (whole grain) with egg 5/8 oz / 200g. (yes)
Aubergine 1/8 lbs - 2oz / 60g. (yes)
Zucchini 1/8 lbs - 2oz / 60g. (yes)
Peppers 1/8 lbs - 2oz / 50g. (yes)
Beef meat 1/8 lbs - 2oz / 50g. (yes)
Garlic 2 pieces / 4g. (yes)
Rapeseed oil 1/8 oz / 5g. (yes)
Basic recipe for a vegetable soup (nutritious) 1/4 cup / 60g. (yes)
Tomato juice 1/3 cup / 75g. (yes)
Oregano fresh 1 pinch / 1g. (yes)
Rosemary 1 pinch / 1g. (yes)
Pepper (ground) 1 pinch / 0,5g. (yes)
Salt 1 pinch / 0,5g. (little)

Cooking instructions:
Boil noodles in plenty of salted water, chill and drain.
Wash vegetables, dice aubergine and zucchini.
Core the pepper and cut into cubes of approx. 1 cm.
Braise garlic, minced beef and prepared vegetables in heated oil, pour in vegetable stock and tomato juice and finish cooking.
Add pasta to the sauce.
Heat the whole and season with the spices and salt.

9.35 Pumpkin soup

Promotes digestion, forcing spleen and stomach, reduces blood pressure, strengthens immune system, prevents cancer, reduces radiation damage, improves digestion, regenerates skin, lowers cholesterol, reduces blood glucose, protects liver.
Cooking time approx. 1 hour
Calories p. portion: 105
3 portions
Allergens:

Quantity of ingredients
Pumpkin 3/4 lbs / 300g. (yes)
Carrot 2 pieces / 100g. (yes)
Potato 2 pieces / 120g. (recommended)
Olive oil 1 table spoon / 10g. (yes)
Onion white 1 piece / 50g. (yes)
Water 1 cup / 120g. (yes)

Parsley 1 table spoon / 7g. (yes)
Anise (Common Fennel) 1 pinch / 1g. (yes)
Salt 1 pinch / 1g. (little)

Cooking instructions:
Add the olive oil to the pan, add the diced pumpkin, diced carrots and potatoes. Roast them shortly, add the finely chopped onion, fill with water, add enough water to cover the vegetables at least 3 finger-widths. Boil at low heat.

Season with sea salt, add small cutted parsley, a pinch of anise (little).

Allow to simmer for about 35 minutes. Then purée the soup and add some water, depending on the consistency of the soup.

9.36 Puréed banana

Eat 2 times a day, regulates gastrointestinal function
Cooking time approx. 7 min
Calories p. portion: 144
1 portions
Allergens:

Quantity of ingredients
Banana 1 piece / 150g. (recommended)

Cooking instructions:
Mix the banana with the fork or purée with a blender. Leave to brown for at least 5 minutes.

9.37 Quinoa piquant with avocado

Anti-inflammatory, good to fight swelling, pain and itching. Reduces blood pressure, strengthens immune system. Strengthens gastrointestinal function, expands blood vessels. Good to fight gastrointestinal complaints.
Cooking time approx. 20 min
Calories p. portion: 561
2 portions
Allergens:

Quantity of ingredients
Water 1 1/2 cups / 240g. (yes)
Quinoa 1 cup / 100g. (yes)
Carrot 1 piece shredded / 100g. (yes)
Onion (spring onion) 2 table spoons (chopped) / 12g. (yes)
Curcuma 1/2 teaspoon / 1g. (yes)
Avocado 1 piece soft / 300g. (recommended)
Salt 1 pinch / 0,5g. (little)
Pepper (ground) 1 pinch / 0,2g. (yes)
Linseed oil 2 teaspoons / 4g. (yes)

Cooking instructions:
Put quinoa in hot water.
Add grated carrot, pepper and salt, finely chopped spring onion and turmeric.
Simmer about 20 minutes, pull from the fire.
Add pre-cut avocado.
Add a dash of oil and sprinkle with fresh parsley.

Spices and herbs: turmeric, cardamom, cress, parsley, chives.

Variation: For those who want more hearty, you can also use a sardine from organic fish preserves. If you are the "protein type", this breakfast will hold on for a long time!

9.38 Radish, apple and yogurt fresh food

Stops diarrhea, promotes digestion, appetizing, detoxifying, supports urination, reduces thirst, prevents cancer,
strengthens body cells, dissolves stagnation.
Cooking time approx. 10 min
Calories p. portion: 77
2 portions
Allergens: G

Quantity of ingredients
Yogurt (natural, 3.5% fat) 5 table spoons / 50g. (yes)
Lemon juice 1/2 teaspoon / 2g. (yes)
Salt 1 pinch / 0,5g. (little)
Pepper white (ground) 1 pinch / 0,1g. (yes)
Radish (white, green, purple-red) 1/4 lbs - 4oz / 100g. (yes)
Apple (sweet) 1 piece / 150g. (yes)
Parsley 2 table spoons / 18g. (yes)

Cooking instructions:
Mix yoghurt with lemon juice, salt and white pepper.

Wash radish and apple, peel and finely grate. Mix with the yoghurt sauce, let it pass briefly. Sprinkle with chopped parsley.

9.39 Red berry with beaters

Calms stomach, strengthens tendons and bones, supports urination, promotes digestion. Strengthens immune system, activates cell metabolism.
Cooking time approx. 15 min
Calories p. portion: 124
2 portions
Allergens: G

Quantity of ingredients
Berries of the season 1 1/2 cups / 200g. (yes)
Grape juice red 1 cup / 200g. (yes)
Sugar molasses 1 table spoon / 10g. (little)
Vanilla 1 pinch / 0,2g. (yes)
Cream (30% fat) 2 table spoons / 20g. (little)

Cooking instructions:
Put berries and red fruits (redcurrants, raspberries, strawberries, blackberries and blueberries) in a saucepan.
Add half a glass of elderberry juice, half a glass of red wine or red grape juice. Add one tablespoon of sugarcane molasses and a pinch of vanilla. Simmer for a few minutes and serve with a bit of whipped cream.

9.40 Red lentils with avocado and radish

Inflammations, promotes digestion, detoxifying, supports urination, reduces thirst. Strengthens heart and kidney, diuretic, calms the stomach, promotes digestion.
Cooking time approx. 20 min
Calories p. portion: 269
3 portions
Allergens: N

Quantity of ingredients
Ginger fresh 2 slices / 2g. (yes)
Water 1 1/2 cups / 200g. (yes)
Lentils red 1 cup peeled / 100g. (yes)
Wakame 1 inch / 1g. (yes)
Salt 1 pinch / 0,5g. (little)
Lemon juice 1 dash / 1g. (yes)
Curcuma 1 pinch / 0,3g. (yes)
Avocado 1 piece / 300g. (recommended)
Pepper (ground) 1 pinch / 0,2g. (yes)
Pepper powder (hot) 1 pinch / 0,2g. (yes)
Sesame oil 1 dash / 1g. (yes)
Radish (white, green, purple-red) 1 cup / 100g. (yes)

Cooking instructions:
Put in a pot with water, some chopped ginger, peeled red lentils, a
piece of wakame or a small amount of hijiki and simmer until the lentils
are soft. Season with salt, lemon juice and turmeric.

Meanwhile: place half an avocado per serving on one-third of the plate:
add ground pepper, a pinch of salt, a little lemon juice, a pinch of sweet
pepper and a little sesame oil.

Put the grated radish on the second plate third.

Fill the lentil dish into the last third of the plate.
Variant: Use radish slices instead of radishes.

9.41 Refreshing cucumber soup with potatoes

Diuretic, detoxifying, suppresses conversion of sugar into fat, lowers
cholesterol, prevents cancer, reduces inflammation, improves digestion,
lowers cholesterol, dissolves stagnation, improves blood circulation,
stimulates appetite.
Cooking time approx. 15 min
Calories p. portion: 148
3 portions
Allergens: GN

Quantity of ingredients
Sesame oil 1 table spoon / 10g. (yes)
Potato 4 pieces / 300g. (recommended)
Onion (spring onion) 3 pieces / 60g. (yes)
Pepper (ground) 1 pinch / 0,5g. (yes)
Nutmeg 1 pinch / 1g. (yes)
Salt 1 pinch / 1g. (little)
Lemon 1/2 piece / 25g. (yes)
Cucumber 2 pieces / 500g. (yes)
Cream, sweet 30% 1 table spoon / 10g. (little)
Dill 1 table spoon / 15g. (yes)

Cooking instructions:
Sauté sesame oil, chopped potatoes, plenty of spring onions in a hot
pot; add pepper, a little nutmeg, salt, lemon juice, hot water, diced
cucumber; simmer for about 10 minutes and then puree; add some
sweet cream as you like, fresh dill.

Variation: Add a little chili, oregano, thyme or rosemary to soften the
cooling effect.

9.42 Rhubarb and apple jelly

Antioxidants, lots of vitamin C, laxative, relieves pain, detoxifying,
warms stomach and spleen, improves blood circulation.
Cooking time approx. 15 min
Calories p. portion: 180
2 portions
Allergens:

Quantity of ingredients
Rhubarb 5/8 oz / 200g. (yes)
Apple juice (natural cloudy) 1 cup / 300g. (recommended)
Corn starch 1 oz / 30g. (yes)
Honey 1/2 oz / 20g. (little)
Vanilla sugar natural 1 pinch / 0,5g. (little)
Cinnamon ground 1 pinch / 0,5g. (yes)
Peppermint 2 leaves / 2g. (yes)

Cooking instructions:
Add the cornstarch to a 1/2 cup apple juice.
Simmer the rhubarb in 1 cup of water for 10 min.

Add the remaining apple juice and the cornstarch, stir, heat till it boils again.
Sweet with honey and season with vanilla and cinnamon. Spread the mixture on dessert bowls and garnish with mint.

9.43 Rice congee with dried fruit

Good to fight blood circulation disorders, diarrhea, antipyretic, high blood pressure, a headache, for the drainage of the body overweight and high blood pressure, stops coughing, supports urination. Provides Vitamin C.
Cooking time approx. 10 min
Calories p. portion: 210
2 portions
Allergens: GO

Quantity of ingredients
Basic recipe for a rice soup (Congee) 4 cups / 500g. (yes)
Butter Bio 1/2 teaspoon / 5g. ()
Apricot dried 6 table spoons / 50g. (little)
Water 1/2 cup / 50g. (yes)
Maple syrup 1 dash / 3g. (yes)

Cooking instructions:
Cook rice congee according to basic recipe.

Melt a small amount of butter over a low heat and briefly fry small dried fruit with 1/2 cup of water. Add the amount of rice porridge desired for the meal and heat. Serve hot and sweeten with maple syrup if necessary.
Variant: In addition fresh fruit with braise.

9.44 Rice with parsnips

Rich in vitamins, minerals potassium and zinc. Good to fight blood circulation disorders, thrombose, risk of embolism, high blood pressure, a headache, heart attack and stroke, yeast infections.
Cooking time approx. 45 min
Calories p. portion: 206
3 portions
Allergens:

Quantity of ingredients
Rice variety any 1 cup / 120g. (yes)
Water 1 1/2 cups / 200g. (yes)
Salt 1 pinch / 1g. (little)
Parsnip 3-4 pieces / 450g. (recommended)
Olive oil 1 table spoon / 10g. (yes)
Sage 1 teaspoon / 3g. (yes)

Cooking instructions:
Peel the parsnips and cut into slices. Fry for a short time in oil. Add the rice and fry again for a short time. Add the water and cook it at least 30 min. Sprinkle with fresh chopped sage.

9.45 Roasted oatmeal with grapes compote

Calms stomach, strengthens tendons and bones, supports urination, promotes digestion. Strengthens immune system, liver and spleen.
Cooking time approx. 25 min
Calories p. portion: 328
2 portions
Allergens: AO

Quantity of ingredients
Oat flakes roasted 1 cup / 120g. (yes)
Grapes red 1 1/2 cups / 240g. (little)
Ginger fresh 1/2 teaspoon / 1g. (yes)
Raisins 2 table spoons / 20g. (little)
Cinnamon ground 1 pinch / 1g. (yes)
Water 1 1/2 cups / 200g. (yes)

Cooking instructions:
Roast the oats briefly, pour over water, add raisins and cook while stirring for 20 min. Add grapes, ginger and cinnamon.

9.46 Rosemary Potatoes

Reduces Inflammation, improves digestion, regenerates skin, supports urination, lowers cholesterol. Rosemary stimulates digestion, strengthens lung, promotes spleen and kidney, dries out.
Cooking time approx. 30 min
Calories p. portion: 188
2 portions
Allergens:

Quantity of ingredients
Potato 6-8 pieces / 420g. (recommended)
Salt (herbal) 1 pinch / 1g. (little)
Olive oil 1 table spoon / 10g. (yes)
Rosemary 1 teaspoon / 2g. (yes)

Cooking instructions:
Cut the potatoes into half's, apply a little olive oil on the cut surface,
then salt, sprinkle 2 - 3 rosemary needles on the potatoes.
Place the potatoes on the baking tray and bake them in the preheated
oven for approx. 25 minutes to 190°C/374°F.

9.47 Rucola salad with tomatoes

Promotes digestion, helps to digest fat, supports urination, reduces
blood pressure, stimulates digestion, strengthens the muscles,
antioxidativ, helps to fight gastritis, flatulence and heartburn.
Cooking time approx. 10 min
Calories p. portion: 129
1 portions
Allergens: O

Quantity of ingredients
Olive oil 1 table spoon / 10g. (yes)
Pepper (ground) 1 pinch / 0,2g. (yes)
Salt 1 pinch / 0,3g. (little)
Vinegar (Apple vinegar) 1 dash / 1g. (yes)
Tomato 4 pieces / 200g. (yes)
Rucola 2 handful / 30g. (recommended)

Cooking instructions:
In a salad bowl stir in olive oil, freshly ground pepper, salt, vinegar and
diced tomatoes; plenty of finely shredded rucola leaves.
Variants: Cut shiitake mushrooms into fine strips: Fry one half in a little
butter and mix with the other half of raw shiitake under the salad. In
place of shiitake mushrooms can be used.
Serve with: toasted bread, polenta.

9.48 Russian kasha with white cabbage

Promotes digestion, relieves pain, detoxifying, promotes digestion, stimulates appetite, dissolves stagnation, stimulates blood production and metabolism, reduces fat.
Cooking time approx. 30 min
Calories p. portion: 250
2 portions
Allergens: AG

Quantity of ingredients
Buckwheat whole grain 1 cup / 130g. (yes)
Water 1 1/2 cups / 240g. (yes)
Nutmeg 1 pinch / 1g. (yes)
Salt 1 pinch / 1g. (little)
Parsley 1 table spoon / 10g. (yes)
Ground 1 pinch / 2g. (yes)
Butter Bio 1 teaspoon / 3g. ()
White cabbage Handful / 20g. (yes)

Cooking instructions:
Roast buckwheat golden yellow; add boiling water, heat till it boils briefly and then let it swell until soft; Grate the white cabbage finely and fold in. Season with nutmeg, a little salt; some parsley, cumin and butter at the end.

9.49 Soup with cucumbers and tomatoes

Diuretic, detoxifying, suppresses conversion of sugar into fat, lowers cholesterol. Promotes digestion, helps to digest fat, supports urination, reduces blood pressure, calms nerves and stomach.
Cooking time approx. 10 min
Calories p. portion: 137
2 portions
Allergens: CO

Quantity of ingredients
Cucumber 1 piece / 300g. (yes)
Tomato 4 pieces (very ripe) / 200g. (yes)
Onion white 1 piece / 50g. (yes)
Peppers 1/2 piece (green) / 10g. (yes)
Salt 1 pinch / 0,5g. (little)
Vinegar (Apple vinegar) 1 dash / 2g. (yes)

Water 1 cup / 120g. (yes)
Chicken egg 2 pieces / 120g. (yes)

Cooking instructions:
Puree all ingredients in the blender. Cool in the fridge. When serving, sprinkle with chopped breadcrumbs and finely chopped boiled egg.

9.50 Spinach with cottage cheese

Improves digestion, regenerates skin, supports urination, lowers cholesterol. Promotes bowel movement, improves blood circulation, forcing spleen and bowel, improves pancreatic function. Strengthens gastrointestinal function.
Cooking time approx. 10 min
Calories p. portion: 263
1 portions
Allergens: GN

Quantity of ingredients
Sesame oil 1 table spoon / 10g. (yes)
Onion white 1/2 piece / 40g. (yes)
Garlic 1/2clove / 1g. (yes)
Spinach 2 handful / 150g. (recommended)
Pepper (ground) 1 pinch / 0,2g. (yes)
Nutmeg 1 pinch / 0,2g. (yes)
Salt 1 pinch / 0,5g. (little)
Sour cream 15% fat 2 table spoons / g. (little)
Potato 4 pieces / 200g. (recommended)
Salt 1 pinch / 0,3g. (little)

Cooking instructions:
Heat in a pot sesame oil, add finely chopped onion, roast glassy; fry a little garlic; stew in strips of spinach for about 3 minutes; add ground pepper, nutmeg, salt, a bit of sour cream as desired or serve the spinach with a large dollop of cottage cheese as an appetizer.
In addition, boil the potatoes in salted water, then peel.

9.51 Spinach with Tahini

Promotes bowel movement, improves blood circulation, forcing spleen and bowel, improves pancreatic function. Improves digestion, regenerates skin, supports urination, lowers cholesterol. Gentle laxative.
Cooking time approx. 20 min
Calories p. portion: 150
4 portions
Allergens: N

Quantity of ingredients
Potato 1,1 lbs / 500g. (recommended)
Salt 1 pinch / 0,2g. (little)
Water 1 cup / 25g. (yes)
Spinach 2,2 lbs / 800g. (recommended)
Sesame paste (Tahini) 2 table spoons / 20g. (yes)

Cooking instructions:
Cook potatoes and peel. Heat water. Blanch spinach. Shake off water and let it dry and stir with sesame.

9.52 Strawberry soup with melons

Relieves pain and inflammation in rheumatism. Diuretic, helps to fight constipation.
Cooking time approx. 5 min
Calories p. portion: 87
2 portions
Allergens:

Quantity of ingredients
Strawberries 3/4 lbs / 300g. (yes)
Strawberry Juice 1/3 cup / 70g. (little)
Lemon peel 1/4 teaspoon / 1g. (yes)
Cantaloupe 5/8 oz / 200g. (yes)

Cooking instructions:
Puree strawberries (fresh or frozen) and strawberry juice with the blender, mix in a little sugar.
Cut melon pulp into small pieces.
Arrange strawberry soup in portions. Put the melon cubes in the sweet soup.

9.53 Sweet-savory barley salad

Diuretic, forcing spleen, supports urination, relaxes. Astringent,
antibacterial, invigorating, calming.
Cooking time approx. 25 min
Calories p. portion: 511
2 portions
Allergens: AGHO

Quantity of ingredients
Water 5/8 oz / 50g. (yes)
Barley 1/4 lbs - 4oz / 100g. (yes)
Apple (sour) 2 pieces / 300g. (yes)
Grapes red Handful / 20g. (little)
Dates dried 2 table spoons (gutted) / 20g. (little)
Almond 1 table spoon / 10g. (recommended)
Curry 1 pinch / 0,2g. (yes)
Salt 1 pinch / 0,5g. (little)
Lemon juice 1 piece / 20g. (yes)
Lemon peel 1/4 piece / 2g. (yes)
Cocoa 1 pinch / 0,5g. (yes)
Cream, sweet 30% 1/2 cup / 100g. (little)

Cooking instructions:
Boil the barley in water.
Mix cooked barley, 2 sweet chopped apples, a handful of red grapes,
about 80 g of pitted dates, about 50 g of chopped almonds, some curry,
a pinch of salt, juice of 1 lemon, grated lemon zest, some cocoa.
Leave for 1 hour;
Lift 100 ml of whipped cream underneath.
Recommendation: in the summer as a refreshing evening meal.

9.54 Tsampa

Promotes spleen, diuretic, forcing spleen, supports urination, relaxes.
Promotes digestion, detoxifying, stimulates nerves, reduces blood
lipids, lowers cholesterol.
Cooking time approx. 5 min
Calories p. portion: 140
2 portions
Allergens: A

Quantity of ingredients
Tsampa (roasted barley flour) 4 table spoons / 30g. (yes)
Green tea 1 cup / 120g. (yes)
Water 1 cup / 120g. (yes)

Cooking instructions:
Tsampa is traditionally made with tea.
The tsampa is poured into a bowl and doused with tea, part of which is drunk and the remainder made into a dough-like mass with tsampa.
You can also pour the tea first; In any case, it takes some skill to achieve the right balance of tsampa and liquid. The two substances are usually mixed with your fingers. It is recommended to add yak butter to improve taste and stability.

9.55 Tsampa with jam or fruit compote

Promotes spleen, diuretic, supports urination, relaxes, stops diarrhea, promotes digestion, appetizing.
Cooking time approx. 5 min
Calories p. portion: 280
1 portions
Allergens: AGO

Quantity of ingredients
Tsampa (roasted barley flour) 2 table spoons / 30g. (yes)
Water 6-8 table spoons / 70g. (yes)
Butter Bio 1/2 teaspoon / 2g. ()
Strawberry jam 1 table spoon / 7g. (little)
Sunflower seeds 2 teaspoons / 14g. (recommended)
Apple (sweet) 1 piece grated / 120g. (yes)

Cooking instructions:
Pour tsampa with boiling water and stir with a spoon until a porridge is formed.
Add butter, jam, sunflower seeds and grated apple.
Sweet to taste with honey, whole cane sugar, or barley malt.
Spices and herbs: fresh mint, vanilla or cocoa, anise, cinnamon

Summer: jam or compote of your choice
Winter: nuts and apple or pear

9.56 Vegetable potato and meat mash

Strengthens immune system, reduces inflammation, improves digestion, strengthens spleen and stomach, strengthens the muscles, tendons and bones, antiparasitic.
Cooking time approx. 30 min
Calories p. portion: 127
2 portions
Allergens:

Quantity of ingredients
Potato 1/4 lbs - 4oz / 100g. (recommended)
Carrot (Early Carrot) 5/8 oz / 200g. (yes)
Beef meat (calf) 1/8 lbs - 2oz / 40g. (yes)
Apricots juice 6 table spoons / 60g. (recommended)
Rapeseed oil 1 table spoon / 6g. (yes)

Cooking instructions:
Remove the flesh, skin, tendons and grease, wash under cool water and cut into small pieces and boil in a little water. After about 15-20 minutes, remove and puree. Wash the vegetables and potatoes, peel and cut into not too small pieces. Cook gently with a little water over a low heat for 10-20 minutes. Use the blender to chop the vegetables. Mix everything, add butter or oil and fruit juice and puree again.

Alternately use other meats such as chicken, lamb or turkey. Also change vegetables with zucchini, kohlrabi, fennel, pumpkin, parsnips and broccoli.

Also change the fruit juices. This can produce a variety of flavors.

9.57 Vegetarian vegetable-cereal-potatoes mash

Improves digestion, regenerates skin, supports urination, lowers cholesterol, supports urination, relieves constipation, strengthens mother milk production.
Cooking time approx. 25 min
Calories p. portion: 91
2 portions
Allergens: A

Quantity of ingredients
Carrot (Early Carrot) 1 oz / 30g. (yes)
Parsnip 1 oz / 30g. (recommended)
Zucchini 1 oz / 30g. (yes)
Fennel 1/2 oz / 10g. (yes)
Potato 1/8 lbs - 2oz / 50g. (recommended)
Water 1/2 oz / 20g. (yes)
Oat flakes (whole grain) 1/2 oz / 10g. (yes)
Orange juice 1 oz / 30g. (little)
Rapeseed oil 1/4 oz / 8g. (yes)

Cooking instructions:
Wash the vegetables and potatoes, dice and fry in a little water. Add water and oatmeal, puree everything and finally add the oil. Note: This porridge replaces the vegetable-potato-meat porridge when meat is to be dispensed with in the infant's diet. Since meat is the best food source for iron, a vegetarian diet must pay particular attention to a sufficient supply of iron.

9.58 Vitamin drink

Regulates gastrointestinal function, promotes spleen and liver, reduces blood pressure, strengthens immune system, prevents cancer, reduces radiation damage, supports urination, quenches thirst, calms the stomach, prevents cancer.
Cooking time approx. 5 min
Calories p. portion: 172
3 portions
Allergens:

Quantity of ingredients
Orange juice 1 cup / 300g. (little)
Carrot 5/8 oz / 200g. (yes)
Banana 2 pieces / 300g. (recommended)
Kiwi 1 piece / 20g. (yes)

Cooking instructions:
Chop oranges, carrots, bananas and kiwi and finely puree with the blender.

9.59 Warming porridge

Strengthens immune system. Diuretic and laxative. Provides vitamin C. Dissolves stones. Promotes digestion, detoxifying, promotes perspiration, reduces blood lipids, stimulates, dissolves stagnation.
Cooking time approx. 10 min
Calories p. portion: 357
1 portions
Allergens: AHO

Quantity of ingredients
Oat flakes (whole grain) 6 table spoons / 60g. (yes)
Fig dried 3 pieces / 15g. (little)
Star anise 1 piece / 1g. (yes)
Ginger fresh 1 pinch / 0,5g. (yes)
Water 1 cup / 120g. (yes)
Maple syrup 1 table spoon / 10g. (yes)
Walnuts 1 table spoon (chopped) / 8g. (recommended)

Cooking instructions:
Soak the dried fruit. Roast Oatmeal dry. Add dried ginger, star anise or cinnamon, a little grated ginger and boil everything with water to a mash. With maple syrup sweet. Whip grated walnuts and sprinkle before serving.

Effect: Suitable for the cold season.
Caution: Fresh ginger does not drink over a long period of time.

9.60 Wheatgrass porridge with pink grapefruit

Little laxative. Promotes digestion. Protects the digestive system. Detoxifying, affects anorexia, good to fight flatulence, inflammatory bowel disease. Warms stomach and spleen.
Cooking time approx. 10 min
Calories p. portion: 398
2 portions
Allergens: AG

Quantity of ingredients
Cow's milk (1.5% fat) 2 cup / 500g. (yes)
Wheat semolina 1/4 lbs - 4oz / 100g. (yes)
Sugar cane sugar 1/8 lbs - 2oz / 40g. (little)
Grapefruit (Pomelo) 1/2 piece / 120g. (yes)

Sugar cane sugar 2 teaspoons / 4g. (little)
Cinnamon ground 1 pinch / 0,3g. (yes)

Cooking instructions:
Put the milk in a saucepan and heat on the stove. If the milk is warm, stir in the semolina with a whisk. Add the sugar. Keep it low and wait until the semolina has absorbed the liquid.

Put in a plate and add chopped crevasses of grapefruit. Sprinkle the porridge with sugar and cinnamon.

10 Effects of food

10.1 Use ingredients: recommendable

Acai powder
Almond
Almond marzipan
Almond milk
Almond puree
Apple juice (natural cloudy)
Apricots juice
Avocado
Banana
Banana (cooking banana)
Berry juice
Bitter Herb liqueur
Blueberry juice
Boletus mushroom
Brazil nuts
Cashews
Champignon
Chanterelle
Cherry juice
Chestnut puree
Chestnuts
Coconut flakes
Coconut grated
Coconut meat
Cream 10% coffee cream
Fox nut, gorgon nut, makhana
Hazelnuts
Hibiscus
Kudzu
Lamb's lettuce
Leaf salads (bitter)
Lettuce
Lily bulbs
Linseed

Linseed (crushed)
Mango juice
Mascarpone cheese
Morel (black, dried)
Morel, dried
Mu Erh Mushroom
Muesli
Parsnip
Peanut (roasted)
Peanuts
Pear juice
Pine nuts
Pistachios
Poppy
Potato
Potato (mealy)
Pumpkin seeds
Reishi mushroom
Rucola
Sesame, black
Sesame, white
Shiitake, dried
Soy flour
Soy noodles
Soya Cuisine (soy cream)
Soybean milk
Soybeans
Soybeans, black
Soybeans, blacks, fermented
Soybeans, yellow
Spinach
Sunflower seeds
Sweet potato
Topinambur

Vegetable juice
Walnuts

Walnuts roasted
Wheat bran

10.2 Use ingredients: yes

Adzuki beans
Agar agar (kelp)
Agrimony
Aloe juice
Amaranth
Amaranth Pops
Anchovy / Sardine
Angelica root
Anise (Common Fennel)
Apple (sour)
Apple (sweet)
Apple puree
Apricot
Apricots
Arrowroot
Artichoke
Asparagus (green or white)
Aubergine
Baking powder
Balm
Bamboo shoots
Banchatee (green tea)
barberry
Barley
Barley flour
Barley grass powder
Barley grouts
Barley malt
Barley not peeled
Basic recipe for a beef soup
Basic recipe for a beef soup (warming)
Basic recipe for a chicken soup
(warming)
Basic recipe for a duck soup
Basic recipe for a fish soup
Basic recipe for a rice soup (Congee)
Basic recipe for a vegetable soup
(nutritious)
Basil
Basil (fresh)
Batavia
Bay leaf
Bean oil
Beans (green, fresh)
Bearberry leaf
Beef bone marrow
Beef fillet
Beef heart
Beef heart (calf)

Beef lungs (calf)
Beef meat
Beef meat (calf)
Beef meatbones
Beef Oxtail pieces
Beef soup meat
Beef stomach
Berries of the season
Bitter orange peel
Black beans
Black caraway
Black fungus mushroom
Black tea
Blackberry dried (unripe fruit)
Blackberry leaves
Blackberry´s
Black-eyed peas
Blackthorn (Sloe)
Blue mallow tee
Blueberry
Blueberry dried
Bocksdorn fruits (Fructus Lycii, Goji,
goji berry dried
Borage
Borage oil
Boxhorn clover seeds
Bread with carob kernel flour
Breadcrumbs (wheat bread, bread roll)
Brie cheese
Broad beans (thick beans)
Broccoli
Brussels sprouts
Buckbean
Buckwheat
Buckwheat (roasted) Kasha
Buckwheat whole grain
Bulgur (cereals)
Burdock root tea
Bush beans
Butter (half fat)
Butter beans white
Buttermilk
Calamari
Camembert
Cantaloupe
Capers in olive oil
Carambola (Star fruit)
Cardamom
Carob flour, St. john's bread

Carp
Carrot
Carrot (Early Carrot)
Carrot juice without sugar
Cauliflower
Caviar
Celery root
Celery sticks
Cereal coffee
Chamomile
Chamomile tea
Channa-Dal
Chard
Chenpi (chinese tangerine bowl)
Cherry
Cherry (sour)
Cherry compote
Chervil
Chervil dried
Chicken Blood
Chicken egg
Chicken egg white
Chicken heart
Chicken meat
Chicken stomach
Chicken yolk
Chickpeas
Chickweed
Chicory
Chili (pod or ground)
Chinese cabbage
Chinese pearl barley
Chives
Chlorella (fresh water)
Chocolate
Chrysanthemum blossom tea
Cinnamon ground
Cinnamon sticks
Clementine
Clementines
Clove
Cocoa
Coconut milk
Cod
Codfish
Coffee
Coix (seeds) YiYi Ren
Cola drink (low calorie)
Compote (fruits of the season)
Coriander
Coriander (fresh)
Corn
Corn (fast polenta)
Corn (roasted)

Corn flour
Corn germ oil
Corn Grease (Polenta)
Corn silk tea
Corn starch
Cottage cheese
Couscous
Cow's milk (1.5% fat)
Cow's milk (whole milk 3.5% fat)
Crab
Cranberries
Cranberry
Cranberry
Cranberry juice
Cream sour 10%
Creamer
Cress
Crispbread
Crucian
Cucumber
Cucumber (bitter)
Cucumber (spicy cucumber)
Cumin (Caraway seed)
Curcuma
Curd cheese 20%
Currant (black)
Currant (red)
Currant (white)
Currants (black)
Currants (red)
Curry
Curry paste red
Daisy
Dandelion (young plants)
Dandelion juice
Dandelionroots tea
Dashi
Dates red
Deer meat
Deer meat
Deer's Bones
Deer's kidneys
Dill
Duck (heart)
Duck (slaughtered)
Ducks egg
Dulse (seaweed)
Dyer's broom herb
Edam cheese
Elderberries
Elderberry blossom tee
Emmental cheese
Endive salad
Evening primrose oil

Fennel
Fennel seeds ground
Fennel tea
Fenugreek (Trigonella foenum-graecum)
Feta cheese
Feta cheese
Fig
Fish innards
Fish pieces mixed (fresh water)
Fish remains
Fish sauce
Flounder
Flower pollen
French beans
Fresh cheese
Fresh cheese from soya
Fresh cheese with herbs
Freshwater crab
Freshwater fish
Fruit tea
Gail plum
Galangal
Garam Masala powder
Garlic
Gelatin white
Gelee Royal
Gentian root
Gentian root tea
Ginger fresh
Ginger oil
Ginger powder
Ginkgo fruit
Ginseng
Ginseng root
Goat
Goat and sheep's blood
Goat and sheep's brain
Goat and sheep's milk
Goat and sheep's stomach
Goat cheese
Goose blood
Goose egg
Gooseberry
Gouda cheese
Gourd
Grape juice red
Grape juice white
Grapefruit (Pomelo)
Grapefruit dried peel
Grapefruit juice
Grapeseed oil
Grass carp
Green spelt

Green tea
Greengage
Ground
Ground caraway
Guava
Halibut (Flatfish)
Hawthorn
Herbal tea mix
Herbs bitter
Herbs of Provence
Herbs various
Herbs wild
Herring
Hibiscus tea
Hijiki
Hokkaido pumpkin
Hop
Horehound leaves
Horse meat
Hyssop
Iceberg lettuce
Jasmine blossoms tee
Jellyfish
Juniper berry
Kaki plum
Kalmus
Kefir
Kidney beans (red)
King Solomon's-seal
Kiwi
Kohlrabi
Kombu seaweed (Saccharina japonica)
Kukicha tea
Kumquats
Lamb bones
Lamb meat
Lamb shoulder
Lamb's lettuce
Lavender blossoms
Leek
Lemon
Lemon Balm (dried)
Lemon Balm (fresh)
Lemon juice
Lemon peel
Lemongrass
Lentils
Lentils black
Lentils red
Lentils yellow
Licorice root tea
Lima beans
Lime
Lime blossom tea

Linseed oil
Liver smoothing tea
Lobster
Longane
Loquate / Japanese medlar
Lotus roots
Lotus seeds
Lovage
Lovage seeds
Luo Han Guo fruit
Lychee
Lychee in Preserved
Lye roll
Mackerel
Mallow (Malva sylvestris) blossom tea
Malt
Mango
Manioc flour
Maple syrup
Mare's milk
Marjoram
Mediterranean fish (cod, plaice, haddock, sea eel, mackerel)
Medlar
Millet
Millet flakes
Mineral water
Mirabelle plum
Miso
Miso black (fermented)
Miso paste (soy bean paste)
Mixed Pickles
Mold cheese
Mozzarella
Mulberry fruit
Mulled Wine Spice
Mullet
Multi-grain bread (gray bread)
Mung bean
Mung bean sprouting
Mussels
Mustard
Mustard Dijon
Mustard medium hot
Mustard seeds
Mustard sweet
Mutton
Mutton
Nasturtium (nose-twister or nose-tweaker)
Nectarine
Nettles
Noodles (wheat) with egg
Noodles (wheat, lasagne) with egg

Noodles (wheat, ribbon noodles) with egg
Noodles (wheat, spaghetti) with egg
Noodles (whole grain) with egg
Nori, purple seaweed, red algae
Nutmeg
Oat
Oat flakes (whole grain)
Oat flakes roasted
Oat flour
Oat fusion (baby food)
Oat meal
Oat milk
Octopus
Octopus
Okra
Olive oil
Olives
Olives green
Onion (shallot)
Onion (spring onion)
Onion read
Onion white
Orange
Orange blossom
Orange dried peel
Orange grated peel
Orange peel
Oregano dried
Oregano fresh
Oyster mushroom
Oyster shell powder
Palm oil
Papaya
Parsley
Parsley root
Passion blossoms tea
Passion fruit
Peaches
Peaches (canned)
Peanut oil
Pear
Pearl barley
Pearl barley
Peas
Peas, green
Pepper (ground)
Pepper Cayenne
Pepper powder (hot)
Pepper white (ground)
Peppercorns
Peppermint
Peppermint tea
Pepperoni

Pepperoni, red, pitted, halved
Pepperoni, yellow, pitted, halved
Peppers
Peppers (rose peppers)
Peppers (sweet)
Peppers powder
Perch
Pheasant
Pickle
Pig blood
Pigeon
Pigeon egg
Pimento
Pineapple
Pineapple (from a can)
Pineapple juice without sugar
Pinto beans speckled
Plaice
Plum
Plum dried
Plums
Pomegranate
Pork Bacon
Pork brain
Pork ham
Pork ham cooked
Pork ham smoked
Pork heart
Pork knuckle
Pork lung
Pork marrow bones
Pork meat
Pork skin
Pork stomach
Pork's intestine
Potato flour
Prickly pear
Processed cheese 12%
Psyllium seed
Pudding powder vanilla
Pumpernickel (dark bread)
Pumpkin
Pumpkin seed oil
Quail
Quail egg
Quince
Quinoa
Rabbit
Rabbit (wild)
Rabbit meat
Radicchio
Radish
Radish (white, green, purple-red)
Radish black

Radish horseradish
Radish leaves
Rapeseed oil
Raspberry
Raspberry dried (immature)
Raspberry leaf tea
Red beet
Red berry (without sugar)
Red cabbage
Rhubarb
Ribworttea
Rice (fragrance)
Rice (Gaoliang / Sorghum)
Rice (whole grain)
Rice Basmati
Rice black
Rice flour
Rice long grain rice
Rice malt
Rice mash
Rice noodles
Rice red
Rice round grain
Rice starch
Rice sticky
Rice sweet
Rice variety any
Rice wild (nature rice)
Romaine lettuce / lettuce salad
Rose blossom tea
Rose hip
Rose hip tea
Rose leaf tea
Rosefish
Rosemary
Rusk
Rye
Rye flour
Rye wholemeal bread
Safflower (Dyer's thistle / Hong Hua)
Saffron
Sage
Sago (cereals)
Sake
Salmon
Salsify
Sauerkraut (cutted cabbage fermented)
Savory
Savoy cabbage / kale
Sea buckthorn
Sea cucumber
Seacrab
Sesame oil
Sesame oil roasted

Sesame paste (Tahini)
Shark
Sheep's milk
Sheep's milk yoghurt
Shrimp
Shrimps
Skim milk powder
Slug
Sorrel
Sour cherries
Sour milk
Sour milk cheese 20%
Sourdough
Soy sauce
Soy Tofu
Soy Tofu smoked
Soybean oil
Spelled (Dark) bread
Spelled flakes
Spelled grain
Spelled semolina
Spelled wholemeal flour
Spiny lobsters
Spurdog (spiny dogfish, Schillerlocken)
St. Benedict's thistle, blessed thistle,
holy thistle, spotted thistle
Star anise
Stevia (candyleaf, sweetleaf)
Strawberries
Sugar fructose - fruit sugar
Sugar glucose - grapes sugar
Sugar Milk Sugar
Sugar substitute (sweetener)
Sunflower oil
Tabasco
Tangerine
Tarragon (Estragon)
Tea mixture uric acid lowering
Thistle oil
Thyme
Thyme dried
Toast bread (whole grain)
Tomato
Tomato dried
Tomato juice
Tomato paste
Tomato puree
Tonic Water
Trout
Trout (smoked)
Truffle
Tsampa (roasted barley flour)
Tuna

Turkey breast meat
Turkey ham
Turmeric (yellow root)
Turnip
Turnips
Umeboshi paste
Umeboshi plums (Japanese apricots)
Valerian
Vanilla
Vanilla pod
Vanilla powder
Vinegar (Apple vinegar)
Vinegar (Red wine vinegar)
Vinegar Aceto Balsamico
Vinegar Aceto Balsamico white
Wakame
Walnut oil
Water
Water hot
Watermelon
Wax gourd
Wheat
Wheat bulgur
Wheat flakes
Wheat flour
Wheat flour whole grain
Wheat germ oil
Wheat semolina
Wheat semolina for children
Wheat/Rye/Gray-black bread with yeast
Wheatgrass juice
Wheatgrass powder
Whey
White beans
White cabbage
Whitefish
Whole grain bread
Wholemeal flour
Wild boar meat
Wild garlic (garlic spinach)
Wild herbs
Wild strawberries
Wormwood herb
Yam root, yam root tuber
Yarrow
Yarrow tea
Yeast
Yew nut
Yoghurt vanilla
Yogi tea
Yogurt (natural, 1.5% fat)
Yogurt (natural, 3.5% fat)
Zucchinix

10.3 Use ingredients: little

Acerola fruit nectar or powder
Agave nectar
Apricot dried
Apricot jam
Apricot nectar
Beef kidney
Beef liver
Beer (alcohol-free)
Beer (alcohol-reduced)
Bitter Lemon
Blackberry jam
Blueberry jam
Bread roll
Brown ale
Chicken liver
Coconut fat
Cranberry jam
Cream (30% fat)
Cream sour 20%
Cream sour 30%
Cream, sweet 30%
Creme fraiche cheese
Curd cheese 40%
Currant jam (black)
Currant jam (red)
Currant juice (black)
Dates dried
Eel
Eel smoked
Fernet Branca (herbal bitter liqueur)
Fig dried
Fructose (glucose)
Fruit mix juice
Ginseng liqueur
Goat and sheep's liver
Goose
Goose fat
Goose parts
Gorgonzola
Grapes red
Grapes white
Honey
Honey wine (Met)
Ladyfingers
Lamb kidneys
Lamb liver

Lychee liqueur
Margarine
Margarine (diet)
Martini
Mayonnaise 50%
Mayonnaise 80%
Orange jam
Orange juice
Parmesan
Pork fat (lard)
Pork kidneys
Pork Lard
Pork liver
processed cheese 30%
Prosecco
Rabbit liver
Raisins
Raspberry jam
Red wine
Rum
Salt
Salt (herbal)
Sherry (whine)
Sour cream 15% fat
Spirit
Strawberry jam
Strawberry Juice
Sugar - icing sugar
Sugar brown
Sugar candy white
Sugar cane sugar
Sugar molasses
Sugar palm sugar
Sugar white
Vanilla sugar natural
Wheat beer
Wheat flatbread/pita bread
White bread (baguette)
White bread (pretzel sticks)
White bread (roll)
White bread (wheat bread)
White breadcrumbs
White dumpling bread (wheat bread cut into chunks)
White wine
Wormwood

10.4 Do not use contra-acting foods

Beer (Pils)
Beer (Top-fermented German dark beer)
Bitter liqueur
Butter Bio
Campari
Chocolate (Diabetic)
Clarified butter
Cola drink

Cooking oil
Oysters
Peanut butter
Pork sausage (Bratwurst)
Contraindicated food
Pork/beef sausage (smoked)
Puff pastry
Supplementary nutrition

11 Herbs and their effects

11.1 Basil

It has a beneficial effect on flatulence and nausea, relaxing and soothing. Good to fight emphysema, bronchitis,
whooping cough, high blood pressure, headache, mouth odor, warts, hiccup, gout, migraine.

11.2 Dill

The medicinal and spice herb has an antispasmodic effect and stimulates gastric juice production. Good to fight flatulence. Antispasmodic for gastrointestinal discomfort.

11.3 Chervil dried

Forces urination, detoxifying, blood-purifying and blood-pressure-reducing effects.

11.4 Coriander

The essential oils are appetizing, digestive, cramping and soothing in stomach and intestinal disorders.

11.5 Chives

Bactericide, prevents cancer, strengthens gastric juice production, promotes digestion and blood circulation, promotes growth, triggers stagnation.

11.6 Lovage

Stimulates digestion, reduces pain. Extracts of the root are used to flush out urinary tract infections and prevent kidney gravel.

11.7 Dandelion (young plants)

Detoxifies, relieves inflammation. Regulates digestion, helps with rheumatism, releases kidney stones, leaves pimples and chronic skin disorders disappear.

11.8 Marjoram

Helps to digest fat foods, strengthens digestive organs, helps to fight colds, strengthens menstruation, promotes skin healing.

11.9 Oregano

It has an anti-digestive, calming and nerve-strengthening effect, helps to fight cramping stomach and intestinal disorders. The ingredient Carvacrol has an anti-inflammatory effect.

11.10   Parsley

Stimulates liver function, detoxifies. Forces urinating. Relieves flatulence. Digestive and menstrual stimulating, birth-accelerating, memory-enhancing, blood-purifying, skin-smoothing.

11.11   Peppermint

Relaxes, frees the lungs and the nose (inhale), regulates the cycle. Stimulates bile flow and bile production, antispasmodic in gastrointestinal disorders, antimicrobial and antiviral.

11.12   Rosemary

Promotes digestion, relieves bloating, strengthens lung, spleen and kidney. Affects the circulation and nerves. Appetizing. Baths help to fight circulatory disorders as well as with gout and rheumatism.

11.13   Sage

Good to fight yeast infections. The leaves have a digestive effect and are used in greasy foods. Antiperspirant effect. Helps to relieve coughing attacks. Dries out (TCM).

11.14   Thyme dried

Disinfecting. It stimulates the blood circulation, increases the appetite and helps to digest fat meat better. Strengthens lungs and spleen (TCM).

12 Basics of Nutrition

The basic principles of nutrition described herein are general recommendations. They are not aimed at a specific form of therapy. Recommendations concerning a therapy have priority.

12.1 Nutrition

Regular meals in a relaxed atmosphere. A warm breakfast is considered a good start into the day.
The main meals ought to be taken for lunch – supper in the early evening. Pay attention to feeling hungry or sated: don't eat too much nor remain hungry is the rule
Prepare the meals freshly from natural, regional products. Frozen, heat-conserved, industrially prepared or foodstuffs cooked in the microwave oven are rejected.
Choice of foodstuffs according to the season: more cooling food in summer, more warming food in winter.
Eat cooked food at least twice a day. Food and drinks ought to be lukewarm, never ice-cold or hot.
Raw vegetables, briefly cooked vegetables, freshly squeezed juices and mineral water are not recommended. Milk and dairy products are only included in the diet if they don't cause problems.
Don't use therapeutic recipes over a longer period without consulting your doctor or therapist.

Varied food
Enjoy the diversity of foodstuffs. Characteristics of a balanced nutrition are variety, suitable combination and a balanced quantity of rich and low energy foodstuffs (on one hand avoiding undersupply with essential nutrients and on the other hand to take to many undesirable substances).

A lot of Cereal Products - and Potatoes
Bread, pasta, rice, cereal flakes (best wholemeal) as well as potatoes contain almost no fat, but many vitamins, mineral nutrients, trace elements, roughage and secondary plant substances. These foodstuffs ought to be taken with low-fat side dishes.

Vegetables and Fruit – „Take Five" every day ...
5 portions of vegetables and fruit a day, as fresh as possible, briefly cooked, or maybe one portion as a juice – ideal as a side dish to every meal as well as snack between meals: Thus a lot of vitamins, mineral nutrients as well as roughage and secondary plant substances

Daily milk and dairy products
Milk and Dairy Products every Day, once or twice per Week Fish;
meat, sausages as well as eggs moderately. These foodstuffs contain
valuable nutrients like calcium in the milk, iodine selenium and omega-3
fat acids in saltwater fish. Meat is favorable due to its high content of
disposable iron and the vitamins B1, B6 and B12. Quantities of 300 – 600
g meat and sausage per week are sufficient. Prefer low-fat products,
especially in meat- and dairy products.

Low-fat and fatty Foodstuffs
Fat supplies us with essential fat acids and fatty foodstuffs contain also
fat-soluble vitamins. Fat is high in energy; therefore much fat in the food
may cause overweight, possibly also cancer. Too many saturated fat
acids may further a tendency for cardio-vascular diseases in the long
term. Prefer vegetable oils and fats (e.g. rapeseed-, olive-, soya-oils and
solid fats produced therefrom). Beware of invisible fat in meat- and dairy
products, pastry and sweets as well as in fast-food and convenience
foods. 70 – 90 g fat per day is sufficient.

Moderately Sugar and Salt
Take sugar and foods/drinks containing various kinds of sugar (e.g.
glucose syrup) only occasionally. Use herbs and spices as well as a little
salt creatively. Prefer salt containing iodine.

Plenty of Liquids
Water is absolutely essential. Drink 1-2 l liquids every day. Prefer water
(with or without gas) and other low-calorie drinks. Alcoholic drinks should
not be taken.

Tasty Dishes, carefully cooked
Cook the meals with as low temperatures and as short as possible, using
little water and fat – this preserves the original taste, keeps the nutrients
intact and prevents the production of harmful compounds.

Take time and enjoy the food
Take your Time and enjoy your Food
Eating consciously helps to eat right. The eye enjoys food, too. It's fun,
invites to enjoy varied dishes and stimulates the feeling of satiety.

Watch your Weight and stay in Motion
A balanced diet and a lot of exercise and sport (30 – 60 min/day) are a
healthy combination. The right weight furthers well-being and health.
Thermals, directional effectiveness, digestive power

There are various criteria for judging the effectiveness of herbs and foodstuffs.

The use of certain herbs and ingredients is based on observations of the effects on the body which these foodstuffs, herbs and spices show after having eaten them. The medical science has developed following system: Every ingredient or herb has a directional effectiveness. Furthermore, there are herbs which have a special effect on certain organs.

The basic condition for a healthy metabolism is to obtain sufficient energy from food and that the digestive process doesn't use too much energy. An easily digestible meal makes content and sated, doesn't cause flatulence and fatigue after the meal. The perfect spices increase the healthiness of our meals. Very often, just small doses of herbs and spices will suffice. They are not used to make us sated, but to help our digestive organs to digest the food.

12.2 Recipes

The recipes list the ingredients to be used and the cooking instructions show how the dish is prepared. The list of ingredients shows the concerned quantities as well as the relevance for the therapy. If you find „less than mentioned", try to comply or find an alternative from the „list of recommended foodstuffs". Mostly it shall result just in a small change of taste when you simply avoid this ingredient.

Mild cooking methods: boiling, stewing, poaching, steaming
Strong cooking methods: barbecuing, roasting, frying, smoking
Balanced cooking methods: deep-frying, baking brick
Deep-freezing and warming in the microwave oven should be avoided (denaturalization).

12.3 Foodstuffs

Foodstuffs have an effect on body and soul like medicinal herbs, only a very much milder one. Dietary advice is mainly based on regional foodstuffs. The knowledge about the effects of each foodstuff and the knowledge, when which foodstuff shall be used, is based on the orthodox school of medicine. Use ecologic-organic products, if possible. As everything should be cooked for a long time due to a better digestability and very rarely eaten raw, the food agrees with everyone.

The classification of the foodstuffs according to their effect on the body is the basis in order to achieve a harmonious status of health.

Dietary advisors do not recommend certain foodstuffs for everyone. The individual diet is tailor-made for the individual constitution.

Buy only fresh and ripe fruit and vegetables. You ought to leave unripe fruit and vegetables and such with brown spots and wilted leaves behind in the market. In this case take deep-frozen goods (never ready-to-serve dishes!). Fruit and vegetables are deep-frozen immediately after harvesting and often contain more vitamins and minerals than the goods from the vegetable shelf. Whereas conserved or tinned goods contain very much less biological substances. Also, salt, sugar and others are mostly added to the latter. Never leave the foodstuffs in the water after washing them to avoid that many vital substances get drowned. Clean salads, fruit and vegetables immediately before serving.

Please make sure of the hygienic processing of foodstuffs. Clean your salads, fruit and vegetables carefully. When cooking with meat, prepare all ingredients first and then process the meat products. Clean the worktop and tools very carefully. Wooden surfaces ought to be treated with a mild disinfectant regularly in order to reduce germination.

Store fruit and vegetables separately, if possible. Harvested fruit and vegetables are still alive and emit e.g. ethylene gas, which makes other products ripen and age faster. Keep meat and fish in the closed packaging or store them in the fridge in closed containers.

12.4 Herbs

There are some basic rules for storing medicinal herbs. On principle, herbs must be protected from direct sunlight, humidity and heat.

Containers for the storage of herbs may be glasses, ceramic jars and even plastic containers. However, plastic is a rather unsuitable material and should only be a short-term solution. In case of glass containers, use a dark material.

Medicinal herbs cannot be kept for any long period. The shelf life of herbs is limited. However, it can be prolonged with suitable storage. The place should be dark, rather cool and absolutely dry. A wooden medicine cabinet, placed not directly next to a source of heat, would be ideal. Never buy large quantities of herbs so as not to have to throw them away. Label the container with the name of the herb and the date of harvesting or processing.

13 Other dietic-books

The following syndromes of dietetics, TCM or for a therapy supplement for cancer are available.

Dietetics

E001. Nutrition of the infant - baby food
E002. Nutrition during lactation
E003. Nutrition in old age
E004. Nutrition of children and adolescents
E005. Nutrition of athletes
E006. Light weight
E007. Pregnancy
E008. Full food

Protein and electrolyte - kidneys
E009. (hemodialysis) dialysis treatment
E010. Acute renal failure
E011. Chronic renal insufficiency
E012. Nephrotic syndrome
E013. Kidney stones (nephrolithiasis)

Gastrointestinal tract - pancreas
E014. Acute pancreatitis (inflammation of the pancreas)
E015. Chronic pancreatitis (inflammation of the pancreas)

Gastrointestinal tract - small intestine and large intestine
E016. Acute obstipation (constipation)
E017. Chronic obstipation (constipation)
E018. Colon irritabile
E019. Diverticulitis
E020. Acquired lactose intolerance (lactose malabsorption)
E021. Fructose malabsorption
E022. Glutensensitive enteropathy (celiac disease)
E023. Colectomy
E024. Short Bowel Syndrome

Gastrointestinal tract - liver, gallbladder, bile ducts
E025. Acute and chronic hepatitis (inflammation of the liver)
E026. Cholelithiasis (bile stones)
E027. fatty liver
E028. cirrhosis

Gastrointestinal tract - Stomach and duodenal intestine
E029. Acute gastritis
E030. Chronic gastritis
E031. Stomach bleeding
E032. Ulcus ventriculi and duodenal ulcer
E033. Condition after gastric surgery

Gastrointestinal tract - oral cavity and esophagus
E034. Stomatitis
E035. Esophageal carcinoma (esophageal cancer)
E036. Refluosophagitis (heartburn)

Special diseases
E037. Phenylketonuria (PKU)
E038. Rheumatic joint diseases

Metabolism
E039. Obesity (overweight)
E040. Diabetes mellitus
E041. Eating disorders (underweight)

Fat metabolism
E042. Hypercholesterolaemia (increased cholesterol level)
E043. Hepatic Encephalopathy

Heart and circulation
E044. Arteriosclerosis (arterial calcification)
E045. Heart insufficiency
E046. Hypertension
E047. Hyperuricaemia and gout

Changed nutrient requirements
E048. In case of fever
E049. For malignant diseases
E050. After burns
E051. Radiation and chemotherapy

CANCER
E100. Pancreatic cancer
E101. Bladder cancer
E102. Blood cancer (leukemia)
E103. Breast cancer
E104. Colorectal cancer
E105. Gastric cancer
E106. Kidney cancer
E107. Esophageal cancer

TCM
E200. Bladder - moisture heat in the bladder
E201. Bladder - moisture and cold in the bladder
E202. Bladder - emptiness and cold in the bladder
E203. Large intestine - external cold affects the large intestine
E204. Large intestine - moisture heat in the large intestine
E205. Large intestine - heat blocks the intestine II acute
E206. Large intestine - dryness of the colon
E207. Large intestine - Yang deficiency (cold)
E208. Heart - Blood insufficiency
E209. Heart - Blood stagnation
E210. Heart - Fire
E211. Heart - Hot mucus clogs the heart pores

E212. Heart - Cold mucus clogs the heart pores
E213. Heart - Qi deficiency
E214. Heart - Yang deficiency
E215. Heart - Yin deficiency
E216. Liver - Ascending Liver Yang
E217. Liver - Blood deficiency
E218. Liver - Blood stagnation
E219. Liver - Moisture heat in liver and gall bladder
E220. Liver - Fire
E221. Liver - Gall bladder Qi-Empty
E222. Liver - Cold in the liver meridian
E223. Liver - Qi stagnation
E224. Liver - Wind
E225. Liver - Wind with ascending liver Yang
E226. Liver - Wind with blood anemic
E227. Liver - Wind with extreme heat
E228. Lung - Qi deficiency
E229. Lung - Mucus-moisture in the lungs
E230. Lung - Mucus-heat in the lungs
E231. Lung - Mucus-cold in the lungs
E232. Lung - Dryness of the lungs
E233. Lung - Wind-heat attacks the lungs
E234. Lung - Wind-cold affects the lungs
E235. Lung - Yin deficiency
E236. Stomach - Bloodstagnation
E237. Stomach - Fire
E238. Stomach - Cold with liquid
E239. Stomach - Nutrition stagnation
E240. Stomach - Qi deficiency
E241. Stomach - Rebellious Qi
E242. Stomach - Yin Emptiness
E243. Spleen - Heat and moisture attack the spleen
E244. Spleen - Coldness and moisture affects the spleen
E245. Spleen - Qi deficiency
E246. Spleen - Qi deficiency + Declining spleen Qi
E247. Spleen - Qi deficiency + spleen does not control the blood
E248. Spleen - Yang deficiency
E249. Kidney - Heart and kidney no longer communicate
E250. Kidney - Jing deficiency
E251. Kidney - Kidneys cannot receive the Qi
E252. Kidney - Qi is not stable
E253. Kidney - Yang deficiency
E254. Kidney - Yin deficiency

For further information visit di-book.com.